FLOWERS
IN EVERY ROOM

FLOWERS
IN EVERY ROOM

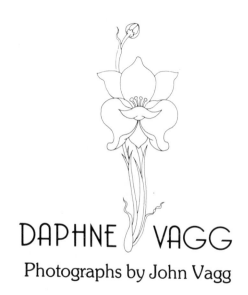

DAPHNE VAGG

Photographs by John Vagg

B.T. Batsford Ltd   London

Frontispiece *The flowers on a side table in a modern Wates Built Home blend well with the setting because they were arranged in situ and the arranger could see the reflection of the room and adjust height, size and colours as needed. The mimosa and daffodils pick up tones in the curtains and napkins and the silvery pussy willows and white chrysanthemums link with the white china. The simple lines of the furniture suggested an unsophisticated arrangement using a basket as the container.*

ISBN 0 7134 4676 5

Typeset by Tek-Art Ltd, Kent
Printed in Italy
for the publishers
B.T. Batsford Ltd
4 Fitzhardinge Street
London W1H 0AH

Acknowledgment

I am happy to record my grateful thanks to Wates Built Homes Ltd., for their kindness in allowing me to arrange flowers, and to photograph them, in their show houses on the Langshott Estate, Horley, Surrey. The furnishings were from Allders of Croydon, and you will see in the frontispiece and in illustrations 4, 6, 7, 8, 13, 16, 17, 19, 20, 25 and 33 what a variety of attractive settings they provided.

To Mr and Mrs K.B. Stork of Mayfield, Deborah and William Brown of Langshott, Horley, Maryann and Anthony Vagg of Royston and Helen and Harold Lowe of Charlwood I record my thanks for the pleasure it gave me to arrange flowers in their homes.

The arrangements in illustrations 15 and 26 were by Beth Hardcastle in her home, Whiligh, in Kent, and I thank her for allowing me to use them.

The rest of the photographs were all taken in my own home.

The photography throughout is by my husband, John Vagg, without whose skill the book would have been nothing. Flowers, colour and decor are visual pleasures which can rarely be described adequately, so the photographs will always be more important than the words.

Daphne Vagg
Mole End, 1984

CONTENTS

PREFACE

The idea for this book came from one of the first programmes I put together for flower arranging demonstrations to clubs, some 15 years ago. I called it 'Accent on Decor' and took with me, to each demonstration, a wallpapered or painted background, a length of fabric and some accessories to simulate a room setting for each arrangement as it was completed.

Interior decor – furnishing styles and the choice of colours, fabrics and woods – has always been an interest of mine and to me the choice of flowers is just as important as any of the others in creating a room which is pleasant to live in. Flower arrangements and their settings need to be compatible, expecially so in the house, so that each brings out the best in the other. The smaller a room is, the more important this becomes.

The immense popularity, in recent years, of flower arrangement as a hobby, or even as a minor art form, has in some ways tended to obscure its more domestic purpose of the pleasure of bringing the garden indoors and making the home look more attractive. Because the art is demonstrated at flower clubs in hired halls, learned at classes in impersonal education centres, staged at competitive flower shows in marquees and used as a fund raiser at festivals in churches and stately homes, the more usual home setting is often overlooked.

Yet most people, most of the time, arrange flowers for their own – or perhaps a friend's – home. They pick from the garden if they are fortunate enough to have one, buy a bunch from the florist, or enjoy the luxury of arranging a birthday or anniversary gift bouquet to grace the dining-table or the lounge or to add a welcome to a guest's bedroom.

So, for the photographs in this book, I have chosen settings in smaller homes, most of them with rooms no larger than those in the average newly built house today. These settings are as important as the flower arrangements and each, I believe, would look less attractive without the other.

INTRODUCTION

History does not precisely record when the first flower arrangement decorated someone's home. We know that Neanderthal man decorated his graves with flowers, but did he decorate his caves with them? Cut flowers are believed to have been used in early civilizations for religious and ceremonial rituals and celebrations, as protection against the plague and evil spirits, or simply as offerings to the gods. Yet the fact that they were decorative, too, could not have escaped our ancestors, or why else did they choose some of nature's most colourful treasures? With rainbows, gemstones and exotic bird plumages, flowers and fruits are certainly among the brightest and most beautiful creations. Mediaeval monks grew bright flowers in their gardens, primarily for culinary and medicinal use, or for the decoration of the church. Did any one of them sneak a small posy of flowers into his cell? For somewhere along the line flowers came into the home, or dwelling-place, to be used as a decoration, pure and simple.

The practice was certainly established in northern Europe by the sixteenth century. Holbein's painting (c.1527) of Sir Thomas More and his family shows roses, lilies, iris, pinks and aquilegias arranged in tall vases in the family home at Chelsea. Dutch and Flemish paintings of interiors of the same period (apart from the grand flower-pieces which could never have existed as actual arrangements but were built up from artists' studies) show small vases of flowers on window sills, cupboards and side tables. Levinus Lemnius, writing from England to his native Holland in 1560, says: 'Although we do trimme up our parlours with green boughs, freshe herbs and vine leaves, no nation does it more trimmely, nor more sightly, than they doe in Englande.' It is interesting that he does not mention actual *flowers* being used, only foliage, and Thomas Tusser in his long rhyming treatise on gardening, published in England in 1573, also fails to mention flowers with his advice: 'Get ivy and hull [holly], woman, deck up thy house.'

In the early seventeenth century, however, John Parkinson, the herbalist, recorded that flowers were brought indoors 'for sight and scent' and that, at a summer party given by the Earl of Dorset, there were 'fresh bowls in every corner and flowers tied upon them and sweet briar, stock, gilly flowers, pinks, wallflowers and any other sweet flowers in glasses and pots in every window and chimney.' Parkinson also wrote of daffodils, 'flagges' (iris), 'yellow larkes spurre' (nasturtium), carnations and thrift being used to 'decke up an house'.

The Elizabethan custom of ornamenting empty fireplaces in summer with displays of flowers, herbs and fruits on a bank of moss continued into the eighteenth century, when the Georgians introduced the bough-pot to stand in the fireplace in summer, holding branches of leaves, blossom and flowers. This was the golden era of English porcelain and pottery factories and many produced vases, wall pockets and bricks with perforated tops

7

specifically designed to hold an arrangement of cut flowers. It is to the Georgians, too, that we owe the fashion which prevails right up to the present day, of using dried leaves, flowers and seedheads for room decoration. Several contemporary writers refer to this practice, and also to the popular habit of growing plants in pots for indoor decoration. Mignonette, carnations, auriculas, campanulas and bulb flowers such as hyacinths and tulips were included.

It was the Victorians, however, who really brought flower decoration into every home in the nineteenth century. Flower arrangement and 'nature study' were among the interests and occupations considered suitable for young ladies in both upper and middle-class homes. All kinds of wild and garden materials, therefore, found their way indoors to be used decoratively in many ways, including being arranged in vases. As with so much else, the Victorians ended up by overdoing this, so that a living room might be decked out with a dozen different vases holding a mixture of flowers, grasses and 'greens'.

The popularity of conservatories and Wardian cases (glazed cabinets, both practical and decorative, in all shapes and sizes, which provided a protected micro-climate) for growing ferns, ivies and other less hardy plants considerably extended the range of plants possible for indoor decoration. The 1980s' revival of interest in terrariums and all manner of houseplants owes much to Victorian origins.

The later Victorian period also produced some of the earliest books about flower arrangement. Annie Hassard's *Floral Decoration for Dwelling Houses* (1870) was probably the first, followed in 1891 by *Floral Decorations à la Mode* by Mrs de Salis. R.P. Brotherston's *The Book of Cut Flowers* appeared in 1906, Gertrude Jekyll's *Flower Decoration in the House* in 1907 and *British Floral Decoration* by R.F. Felton, a London

1 *Flowers and fruit in a tall urn capture something of the classical restraint which the Georgians admired, yet suggest the richness and quality which were also characteristic of that period.*

2 *A Victorian-style table decoration in an epergne of pink glass with barley-sugar twists uses trailing ferns, roses, pinks, carnations and laurustinus.*

florist, in 1910. Each gives a most interesting insight into the ways in which flowers were used in the home.

The Edwardian period, with Art Nouveau influences and a growing interest in oriental styles, brought a greater elegance to flower arrangement and a certain natural restraint after the Victorian clutter. Queen Alexandra, when she was Princess of Wales, was reported to have 'large vases of common beech boughs in the drawing room of Marlborough House'.

After World War One, in the 1920s,

generally regarded as the beginning of the 'modern' era in design and interior decor, flower arrangement was accepted as a normal, everyday part of the decorative indoor scene. For the most part flowers were arranged fairly naturalistically in tall vases and jugs or in low bowls for shorter-stemmed flowers.

In 1929 Anne Lamplugh in *Flower and Vase* was writing that 'a year or two ago the majority of people used only one kind of flower to a vase and this limited the scope of their colour blending very drastically. But lately the vase containing two and even three different kinds of flowers is growing in popularity.' Constance Spry was soon to enlarge on this considerably, bringing into use for house decoration every kind of plant material – lichened branches, fungi, cabbages, root vegetables and unusual seedheads as well as exquisite flowers and colourful leaves. By the end of World War Two, books by Julia Clements and Violet Stevenson were encouraging every housewife and home lover to look at new (and old) ways of bringing flowers indoors for decoration and to regard this kind of occupation as a creative hobby, not merely a simple means of decorating the house.

Paradoxically, it was the upsurge of new flower arrangement clubs in the 1950s and 1960s which ultimately led arrangers away from flowers in the home to flowers in shows, in church flower festivals and in exhibitions in stately homes. That an association such as NAFAS (National Association of Flower Arrangement Societies of Great Britain) should be so outward looking and so involved in money-raising for charities is to its eternal credit, but today's flower arranger is sometimes in danger of being so busy elsewhere that he/she has no time to do the flowers at home! There will always be time, I hope, for both.

3 *Party flowers on a patio or terrace can make a bold talking-point, but they need not be expensive and can include many bits and pieces from the garden. (See page 30.)*

ONE

GUIDELINES

Arrange the flowers where they are to stand

If there is one golden rule about arranging in the home which I suspect most of us ignore, it is that whenever possible flowers should be arranged *in situ*. You may argue that it is better to make the mess (and flower arranging can be messy, let's be honest) in the kitchen, or garage or, if you are lucky, special flower room. So it is: do the messier preparation of stems, container and mechanics, conditioning and bucketing in water there, but do the actual final arranging in the room and on the spot where the arrangement will stand.

The reasons are many:

* Only on the spot can you truly judge the height, width and shape you need. An inch or two more or less can make so much difference to the finished creation.

* You can get the feel of the character of the room. However well you think you know your own house (and most of us have cleaned and tended every corner of it), with flowers to arrange you adopt a quite different attitude, seeing the room as a whole, moving this chair a little to one side, tweaking the curtains straight, deciding that the lamp would really look better on the other side of the bookshelves, and so on. You are *designing* – or redesigning – and the flower arrangement will be the finishing touch and an integral part of the decor of the whole room.

* You can see the colours of the decor and furnishings accurately and you will sense when a particular colour of flower 'does nothing' for the room (and take that colour elsewhere in

the house) or when something is needed to sharpen the colour scheme or pick up a tint or tone that is missing. You can try out a colour, retain or abandon it and adjust, as you go along, to the needs of the colours already in a room. It was Ruskin who wrote: 'Colour is wholly relative – everywhere throughout your work is altered by every touch you add in other places.'

* You can appreciate how the light falls from the windows, whether it is from the left or the right and whether it is much affected by the reflection of green trees, or a brick wall or shadows cast outside. If you arrange in another room where the light comes from a different side and at a different angle, you will unconsciously adapt to it and perhaps get the colour balance quite wrong for the arrangement's final setting.

* You can judge the actual angle of viewing: how the arrangement looks as you walk in the door; how it looks when you sit down; if the back is reflected in a mirror or window and looks untidy; whether it will be in full sun for a large part of the day and so wilt quickly; and whether a taller or lower or different-coloured container would look better.

Get into the habit of taking a sheet of plastic or newspaper to work on and when the arrangement is complete the rubbish can be gathered up in one go.

The room setting should enhance the flowers and the flowers should enhance the room

Flowers should not self-consciously proclaim

(except possibly for a party occasion) 'Look, I am a flower arrangement' any more than you would expect a cushion, a picture or a lampshade to 'announce' its identity. Each of these may, in its own right, be a focal point or accent in a room, but to be effective it has to belong and not stick out like a sore thumb. The analogy with the cushion can be carried further. A brilliantly coloured one can be an effective accent in a room, but not if it is the *only* orange thing in an otherwise beige-neutral-brown room. Some other orange, or near-orange, items need to be included in the furnishings or ornaments to give rhythm and colour-linking through the whole room. So it should be with a flower arrangement. A red one in a room otherwise devoid of red or any red-based tint or tone will be self-consciously ill at ease, taking too much of the limelight, and throwing the whole colour scheme out of balance.

Colour is the most important consideration

Following on from the last point about colour, do not be afraid to experiment. It is often surprising what colour combinations actually work in any given setting. Studying a colour wheel for harmonies and groupings may help, but it often needs a highly trained eye to translate these into flower-petal colourings which are shaded, streaked, edged and backed with different shades, tints and tones and with additional accents of stamens and stem colours. It is far easier for most people to bring a flower in and try it out in an arrangement. You will often find that a touch of pink here links up with a leaf marking there, or the yellow of one flower is echoed by the darker shade of the centre of another, and these in turn will pick up a secondary colour in curtains or carpet. The world of colour has infinite nuances and exciting contrasts and accents. The flower arranger has an unequalled range available at various seasons of the year and one of the greatest delights of arranging flowers at home is accidentally coming across attractive colour combinations.

Grow and buy for your own colour schemes

It is often surprising how little those with gardens bother to grow flowers, leaves and berries with colours which will enhance and complement the colour schemes they have in their homes. It is surely worth a little trouble, when choosing what to grow, to find a rose, a tulip or a berrying shrub which will be useful – really useful – for cutting for particular rooms. The choice today is so wide and there is such a range of colour, size and hardiness of almost every garden plant, that it does pay to study catalogues and to shop around for the ideal. Most of us do not change our furnishings so often that what is planted today will be the wrong colour by the time it reaches cutting proportions.

For those who have to rely on shop flowers, do not be afraid to take with you a piece of fabric or wallpaper or a paint colour card to help you with your choice. Shop assistants are too often inclined to assert that this colour will, or will not, go with that. The choice is yours, so have with you anything which will help. Reaction to a colour is such a personal thing and only you know exactly what you intend to do with it and put with it. The same applies to containers. In the long run, however many containers we possess, there are only a very few in regular use and these usually end up in the same position over and over again. They are tried and trusted. If you have a container which is the right shape and size but the wrong colour for a certain spot, do not hesitate (unless it is a valuable antique, of course) to paint or spray it in a more useful colour. Car retouching sprays are usually translucent enough to tone down an over-bright colour without altering it too much, or a mixture of several sprays can completely change the colour and texture.

4 *The pink and plum colourings in a modern kitchen were the basis for this grouping of flowers, fruit and vegetables in similar and toning colours. It is reminiscent of some of the smaller arrangements found in seventeenth-century Dutch paintings of table-pieces.*

A useful guideline in buying any container or fabric for covering a base to use with flowers is always to go for the greyed tone rather than the clear, full colour.

Next to colour, consider style

Style is, perhaps, a less obvious or precise factor to consider than colour. We are all well aware of the difference between a massed traditional arrangement with lots of flowers and foliage and the sleek modern 'job' with three stalks, two leaves and a dahlia. Some of the in-between styles are not so easily defined, but do attempt to assess each room's character and try to suit any flower decoration to it.

Few of us go all out for, say, an authentic Victorian setting complete in every detail, but we may have a room with pieces of Victoriana which give it a decidedly nineteenth-century atmosphere, and a period-style arrangement using the fussy flowers, ferns and trailing foliages of the time will suit the room well. The pine-furnished room with check curtains will look far more at home with simply arranged garden flowers in a jug than with an elaborately contrived arrangement of orchids and carnations, however well the colours tone. The latter arrangement would be far more suitable for a highly decorative Georgian-style interior than would a concoction of driftwood and bold leaves. There can be no hard and fast rules, but be sensitive to a room's character when choosing a style of arrangement to enhance it.

Care and after-care

Just because an arrangement will be in the house and near at hand for topping up the water, do not delude yourself into thinking that its preparation can safely be skimped. There is no substitute for the long, cool drink for flower stems after cutting, nor the submerging of leaves (except grey ones) under water for at least a couple of hours. Spare time to strip stems of unwanted leaves, snags and thorns *before* giving this long drink or submerging, as this gets rid of so much of the messy rubbish in the garden, kitchen or workroom. Later when you go to arrange *in situ* you will not need to take a lot of unnecessary material with you into a tidy room, and the whole process of creating an arrangement can be pleasurable and uncluttered.

Get into the habit of two-thirds filling the container with water before you start arranging. This helps to give weight and stability to the container and if you do forget to top up with water when the arrangement is finished, no great harm will be done. But again, get into the habit of topping up with water at once. Fill the container to within about half an inch of the top, for it is astonishing how much water an arrangement will drink in the first 24 hours.

Top up daily, and when you can, give a misting spray of water to keep the atmosphere moist around the arrangement; remember to protect polished surfaces when you do this.

When the beauty has faded, get rid of the arrangement. Don't hang on for another day or so because not all the flowers are quite dead. If they are not still beautiful or attractive, they are no longer decorative and should go. A drooping, crumpled, faded flower arrangement is a sad, sad thing.

TWO

ROOM BY ROOM

Each room in a home has its own purpose and gradually, through its colour scheme and furnishings and the objects put into it, develops its own style and, though this is less definable, its own character. A flower arrangement is the final touch, the changeable accessory, the never-to-be-repeated ornament – for even if similar flowers or leaves are used again in the same season next year, they will be subtly different.

Gertrude Jekyll in *Flower Decoration in the House* (1907) observes 'how, after a time, the room "finds itself" . . . how there are certain places where flowers always look well, so that one always puts a vase of flowers there . . . . By degrees one gets to know the want of every room so that in the end the . . . search for flowers is governed by certain limitations, and the quest is thereby simplified.'

Hall and stairway

How many of us, nowadays, have halls large enough to accommodate the 'welcoming arrangement' we are always urged to provide for visitors and callers? Most modern houses are designed to give maximum space to the living-rooms and kitchen so that the hall, in many homes, has become little more than a passageway to the staircase and front door. Older houses that once may have had sizeable halls have often had pieces taken out of them to provide a downstairs cloakroom, shower or utility room. Central heating has meant that possibly the only stretch of wall where a table, chest or cupboard could stand is now occupied by a radiator and that precludes the use of fresh flowers nearby or above for at least half the year when the heating is on.

With little or no room for occasional furniture or even shelving, the answer, maybe, is to look to the walls, to see what can be hung on them.

The wall sconce is a very useful solution. The one in photo 5 is home-made from hardboard (the back) and 12 mm (½ in.) chipboard (the shelf). The back is outlined with a fine cord and decorated with a plastic stick-on motif. A hanging loop of wire must be securely fixed to the back. The whole thing is sprayed with gold paint, including a square tin cut down to make a container about 5 cm (2 in.) deep to stand on the shelf. It emulates a brass eighteenth-century candle sconce which in those days provided room illumination. The candlelight was reflected in the brass back, so providing two-candle power from the light of one.

The arrangement also provided an interesting colour challenge. The walls were a deep burnt orange and the only flowers available from the garden were the pale pink blossom of *Weigela florida* 'Variegata' and one orange 'Whisky Mac' rose. The solution was to buy two sprays of chrysanthemums, one pale tan (almost the same colour as the rose), the other a deeper rust and a bunch of pinks in a bright, deep pink. By choosing a variety of tints and shades that all have some basic red in them, a happy colour link can be made.

Another solution in a small space is a

15

hanging pressed-flower picture or a collage. The three-dimensional collage in photo 6 is unglazed and is made of shells and dried and preserved plant material glued to a hardboard base about 30 × 75 cm (12 × 30 in.). The hardboard was first covered with deep blue-green fabric. Several cut-out shapes of lime-green nylon net, and one or two pressed leaves, were glued (with just the merest touch of glue applied with a cocktail stick) to the background, then the whole board was covered again with the lime-green net. This helped to give a three-dimensional, under-water effect. Seashells provide most of the base shapes and also the 'bubbles' rising towards the top. Seaweed curls, cones, seed-heads, grasses, dried leaves and a lichened twig were built up into a seascape which has lasted a long time with only an occasional blow and a flick with a soft paintbrush to keep it looking fresh.

Lounge or sitting-room

I have always disliked the ugly word 'lounge' preferring the more old-fashioned 'sitting-room'. It is, after all, the room where the family *sits*, whether to talk, read, knit, listen or watch television. Flowers here will probably be the most important in the house; this is where you will put the biggest single arrangement and the

5 *A wall sconce holding flowers is a useful way of raising an arrangement out of the way in a hall or landing where there is continual through-traffic.*

most expensive flowers. The main link with the room decor is likely to be by colour, but style must also play an important part.

Of the sitting-rooms illustrated, the one in photo 7 is a fairly traditional room with neutral beige walls and matching floor-length curtains. An accent of colour is in the blue and green of the faintly oriental settee covering. The brass lamp and dark wood coffee table are quietly toning. The obvious choice of colours for flowers would have been the blue and green of the fabric, but this was spring time with silver pussy willow and white thorn blossom available in the hedgerows and daffodils in the garden. So flowers were bought to extend the yellow-orange colours of the daffodils into the tan and rust ranges, making a warmer group of colours altogether and using hues complementary to the fabric yet without very strong contrasts to upset the balance of the traditional atmosphere of the room. The arrangement is traditional in style as well, in a low, deep yellow bowl.

Compare this with the brilliant contrasts of red, white and blue in the more modern sitting-room (photo 8). With such vivid, primary colouring it is usually better to let one colour be dominant. Here it is the scarlet of the suite. The flowers did not need to compete, simply to 'echo', and four brilliant red polyanthus plants in a white Casa Pupo bowl provided the answer. They are long-lasting, the buds coming out in succession, and when flowering is over they can be planted outside in the garden. Both these arrangements fit quite quietly into their setting, echoing the colour, underlining the room style and character.

Photograph 9 suggests a quite different decorative treatment. The 'tree' of dried leaves, flowers and seedheads plays a very dominant role in a room already full of interest with an eighteenth-century display cupboard, a panel of closely set pictures, books and a flowered carpet. The decor style is almost cluttered, as befits the Victorian button-back chair.

Nevertheless the tree itself could be varied to suit all kinds of rooms and all types of decor. To make the tree trunk a branch of silver birch about 1.3 metres (4½ feet) long is set in cement in a 25 cm (10 in.) diameter plastic flower pot. Two blocks of dry-foam (the brown kind) wrapped in small-mesh wire netting are impaled on the trunk and securely wired or taped. The whole thing can stand in a decorative cache-pot or basket. Then you can have a grand time sorting out your boxes of dried and preserved treasures, wiring them if necessary, to stab in all over the foam, gradually building up a more or less circular tree. It will depend what you have or what you decide to buy. I used pressed ferns and dried hydrangea heads to cover most of the mechanics, then put in stems of silver honesty 'pennies', pressed bracken and fern, artichoke heads, acanthus, broom, butcher's broom, statice, glycerined lady's mantle (alchemilla), dried strelitzias, glycerined bells of Ireland and anything else that came to hand, trying to keep the whole tree light and airy. The large red baubles, impaled on wooden skewers, and one or two glittered sprays, were a concession to Christmas.

In the New Year the baubles were removed and sprays of wired dried mimosa balls were put in instead. The change was quite magical and spring-like and the tree was not dismantled and packed away until spring flowers had become plentiful (and with some regret even then). This type of tree can fit into any season and looks effective with any decor if thought is given to the colouring. In autumn it can be charming with turning leaves and berries and apples instead of baubles on sticks, though you will of course need to use soaked (green) foam and wrap it in thin polythene underneath the wire mesh, to help preserve moisture. In winter, with evergreens (clipped over with shears) and oranges and lemons on sticks, the citrus smell is delicious, and the whole thing takes on a Renaissance look.

6 *A collage of pressed and preserved leaves and seedheads makes a decorative feature which takes up no floor space in a small hall.*

7 *A traditional arrangement in toning colours for the coffee table in a traditionally furnished room.*

Dining-room

Dining-rooms today are seldom the large family rooms they were some 50 or 100 years ago. A dining area may not, in fact, be a separate room at all and is frequently part of an all-purpose family living-room or an annexe to the kitchen.

Flower arrangements, then, are normally concentrated on the table and this means they can be linked to the colour and style of the china and linen, or perhaps to the occasion of the meal if it is a special one, such as an anniversary, Easter, Thanksgiving or Hallowe'en. The general style and colour of the room is less important since those seated at the table for a meal will have the table-setting, rather than the walls, in their line of view. Attractive and imaginative table decorations are possible, although the British tend, as a nation, to be conservative over table arrangements.

Nevertheless, the two settings shown in photos 10 and 11 are very different in style and purpose. The mixed summer flowers in a white china compote, with Booth's 'Floradora' china, decorate a tea table for two, itself almost a thing of the past; so few of us sit down to tea nowadays. The olde-worlde, romantic look of flowers is obtained from using roses, petunias, phlox, marjoram, love-in-a-mist, honeysuckle and everlasting pea in a loose, airy style which echoes that of the flowers on Granny's milk jug. Colour is picked up in the table napkins and the soft green cloth makes a perfect foil. The effect is unashamedly pretty and the two sitting down to their tea could momentarily, at least, be carried back to a more gracious age.

A busy family breakfast table in a modern home with polished pine furniture gets quite different treatment. The brightly patterned yellow place-mats with orange napkins and modern pottery cups and plates are complemented by a bunch of mixed daffodils in an openweave basket. The flowers are actually arranged in a clear glass casserole (which hardly shows), holding loosely crumpled wire mesh to support the stems. This avoids the flowers flopping around the edge of the bowl leaving a gap in the middle, which is what happens when no support is used. An alternative, if no wire mesh is available, is to have a jam jar or smaller, slightly taller vase standing in the middle of the bowl to support some of the taller, central stems. For all its apparent casualness, the arrangement was done with care, though it did not take long. The flowers face in all directions so that everyone at the table has a good view and each daffodil has enough space to show off its best face or profile. A few leaves helped to provide a contrasting shape and the several different varieties of daffodils ensured sufficient interest. Who could wish for a more cheerful start to the day, even if the flowers did have to be removed to the sideboard because Father's propped-open newspaper was crushing them!

Bedroom

Guests are delighted to have a few fresh flowers in their room. Photograph 12 shows just such a welcoming arrangement in an oriental-style basket which links up with the picture. These are snippets from a winter garden: grey catkins of *Garrya elliptica*, starry yellow flowers from winter jasmine and sweet-smelling pink ones from *Viburnum fragrans*, ivies, heather, rosehips, snowberries, yellow holly berries and wired sprays of small cones. This kind of bowl on a mild day in December is as welcome in its way as the more luxurious bowl of July roses in a charming Georgian-style bedroom (photo 13). The gentle colouring on walls and bedspread of white, pale blue and green is picked up in the flowers: 'Iceberg' and 'Boule de Neige' roses with blue love-in-a-mist, mauve catmint and a few heads of wild Queen Anne's lace, all casually

8 *In a vivid red, white and blue setting, polyanthus planted in a white bowl match the red of the modern suite.*

arranged (in crumpled wire mesh) in an old vegetable dish patterned in similar colours. The whole effect is very English and one can imagine the hum of bees and summer scents wafting in through the open window. The white bows to suspend the pictures, the cupid lamp base and frilled cushions complete an essentially feminine room.

If bedroom arrangements are too large they can become cloying and when someone is ill it is especially important to avoid very strong scents. Emphasis can be on soft pretty colours and, if possible, some unusual flowers or pieces of plant material to create interest and a talking point.

It used to be thought necessary to remove flowers from a bedroom at night because they gave off carbon dioxide; the problem was always what to do with them and where to put them. Now they can remain happily *in situ*, and there is no need to change the water daily; it is enough to top up the water level. Gentle misting sprays of warm water (take care to protect the furniture) will keep a bowl or posy fresh for a long time.

If a bedroom arrangement is not possible, have a specimen vase with just one flower. It does make a guest feel welcome and there is no reason why you cannot pamper yourself this way. As a guest, I have been greeted, on various occasions, with two simple sprays of variegated ivy, a miniature vase of tiny silk flowers, a Victorian shaving mug of dried pink helipterums and a flowering stem of *Daphne odora* and each has made me feel special. In this case one flower is certainly worth a thousand words.

Bathroom

Bathrooms used to be bleak and chilly places, especially in winter, with forbidding white tiles, white porcelain baths and basins and cold linoleum on the floor. I doubt if anyone really put flowers in them. Today they are colourful and cosy, even luxurious, with deep-pile carpets to cosset bare feet, patterned ceilings to gaze up to when soaking, or crisp, pretty shower curtains for those who prefer a brisk shower. Pot plants abound, liking the warm, steamy atmosphere.

If you have room a grouped display of plants, or tiers of them on shelving, can soon produce today's popular jungle look! When it comes to arranging cut flowers and foliage, it is likely that bathrooms only get a look in when the colours in the garden seem right, as in photo 14. The stately artichoke opens its mauve-blue flowers at the same time as the round blue globe thistle (*Echinops ritro*), annual poppies (the lovely double mauve one looks as if it is made of tissue paper) and buddleia. Lacy ferns, yellow privet and grey cut-leaved *Cineraria maritima* complete an arrangement which echoes in deeper tones the colours of the wallpaper without actually trying to copy any part of it. The soft green of the glass jar, washbasin and tiles all tie into the colour scheme.

If this kind of arrangement seems too impractical with family use of the bathroom, try a shallow dish or basket of pebbles and shells with one or two sedums, echeverias or perhaps even a cactus or two. Air plants, various forms of *Tillandsia*, have become very popular of late and are suitable for the bathroom. Many need no soil, only regular mist-spraying. Fix the plant with a spot of adhesive to driftwood, shells or a branch, or group several on a shallow basket, rush mat or a decorative tile.

Kitchen

Fruit and vegetables are so colourful and varied in texture that one would expect them to be far more widely used for decoration than they are. Think of the clear shiny reds of tomatoes, apples and peppers; the cool yellow of lemons, grapefruit and bananas; the bright orange of carrots and oranges themselves; the

23

10 *Tea for two in high summer, with an olde-worlde posy of mixed garden flowers in soft colourings.*

11 *Daffodils massed in a low basket on the breakfast table give a cheerful start to the day.*

12 *An oriental basket of snippets from a winter garden makes a guest-room especially welcoming.*

13 *White roses and love-in-a-mist accentuate the femininity of this Georgian-style bedroom.*

26

soft, muted bloom of peaches, plums and apricots, rough-textured pineapples, coconuts, cauliflowers and potatoes; matt and shiny nuts; ridged celery and smooth bunches of grapes. The one drawback is that most of them are round, or very nearly so. Other shapes of plant material are needed with them in an arrangement to give variety.

The grouping here on a large basketry base in a blue and white kitchen shows a varied choice of foliage. Spears of New Zealand Flax (*Phormium tenax*) contrast with finely cut yew and rosemary, large shiny leaves, the rough flower heads of artichoke, smooth, bright oranges and lemons and soft, bluish plums. A few spikes of lemon-yellow gladioli carry the colour up into the design.

Many kitchens will not have room for a large arrangement like this, but most will have some spot where a small grouping of items normally in the kitchen can form a pleasing still life. A tray, a shallow basket, a pastry or cutting board, a copper pan or an iron trivet all seem compatible as bases or containers; bottles, peppermills, jars, jugs, moulds and a pestle and mortar may make useful accessories. For those without space even for this, put the cut herbs (mint, marjoram, fennel, chives) waiting to be used into an attractive little jug to decorate the window sill. This is a good place, too, for the houseplant or rooting cutting that needs special attention; constantly under your eye as you wash up or prepare vegetables at the sink, it will repay you for t.l.c. (tender, loving care) and become decorative again. But put it in a pretty cache-pot or bowl or basin while it is in intensive care and help it to look its best.

Study

By tradition the study has been a male preserve – a den for the master of the house where he could retire for quiet reading and writing away from the family hubbub. Today it is more likely to be an office for the man who works from home or the woman who does a part-time job at home involving typing, writing or accounts.

In either case it is a room to work in and decor and flowers should be quietly stimulating rather than too soothing, pretty and restful, or the worker may fall asleep.

This attractive small room in a modern Wates Built Home has a simple decor of black, white and grey, sharpened with one or two accents of scarlet. There is an oriental atmosphere about its sophisticated simplicity, emphasized by the lacquered look of the black wood and red paper rack, the shape of the desk handles and the 'Chinese Chippendale' touch in the chair back. A Japanese-style flower arrangement (ikebana) could obviously carry this further.

I chose instead to make a very simple Western-style arrangement in a hand-thrown glazed black pot with three chimney-like openings at the top. The dried matt-black-sprayed strelitzia leaves had formed their own interesting curves to make a pleasing outline. The room's red accent is repeated in clustered red carnations which provide their own rough-looking texture as a contrast to the smooth wood, plastic and glass of the prints on the wall. It is interesting to note how the room designer has kept these and the curtains very understated to give a greater illusion of space and to leave the desk as the focal point of a small room.

Patios and terraces

More and more, we are making living spaces outside the house for summer sitting, for meals and for parties. If you can have a party out-of-doors (and the wind is not too bothersome) it is a splendid opportunity to make flower and fruit arrangements on a larger scale than may be possible indoors.

The late summer buffet arrangement shown on page 10 combines all kinds of garden treasures – red hot pokers, crocosmia, acanthus seedheads, ivy, berries, geraniums, gourds – and fruits bought in the supermarket. A large, deep, dinner plate stands on an upturned shallow basket. Two pieces of floral foam are anchored and taped to the plate; a tall block at the back and a half-block in front. They need to be very secure as the whole arrangement is quite heavy when finished and people will be moving about nearby, so it must be stable. The height is given by several hollow green stems of *Leycesteria formosa* to which the ivy and grapes are fixed. Other stems are held in the foam and each fruit is impaled on a wooden kebab skewer which acts as a stem. Heavy fruits (such as melon or pineapple) may need two or even three skewers to take their weight. There are really no rules for a build-up like this. Almost anything goes, but because it was out-of-doors and, in this case, in front of a white-washed, ivy-clad wall, nothing too sophisticated was needed. Such a decoration needs to be bold and eye-catching.

16 *A bold arrangement of black-painted leaves and scarlet carnations repeats the strong colour contrasts in a small study.*

THREE

COMPLEMENTING THE DECOR

Traditional rooms

The two most popular traditional, or period, styles in recent years to have affected interior decor, even in modern houses, have been Georgian and Victorian. 'Tudorbethan', as it was once amusingly dubbed, has been out of favour of late, but is making a come-back and nostalgia for the 1920s and 1930s has brought back some Art Deco styles.

For the most part, unless one is the fortunate owner of antiques, period style is achieved with reproduction furniture and by borrowing or adapting decorative features such as marbling, carved pine or white-painted fireplace surrounds, fire baskets, mahogany, walnut and elm wood finishes, wallpapers copied from earlier designs, curtain poles and Regency-style brass handles, finials and inlays. These may produce no more than a suggestion of period style, but with flowers to suit, the atmosphere can be strengthened.

It is no accident that roses are used in both photographs 17 and 18 of traditionally furnished rooms, for roses belong to every historical period from Ancient Rome to the present day. Yet they retain an 'Englishness' which is hard to define, especially when arrangements in June can include some of the old-fashioned varieties.

The bowl by the Georgian-style fireplace in photograph 17 includes *Rosa mundi*, 'Fantin Latour', 'Pink Perpetué', 'Handel' and 'Lilian Austin' roses. They are arranged, with plenty of their own leaves, in crumpled wire mesh as a support, in a rose-patterned china bowl. The various pinks pick up and enhance the deep pink velvet upholstery, the marble veining in the fireplace and the tones in the print of the eighteenth-century conversation piece.

The roses (photo 18) arranged in two shallow containers (this time in floral foam as a stem support) on the library steps by the bookshelves include similar varieties with foxgloves (*Digitalis*). Neither room is strongly 'period', nor are the arrangements, yet each is traditional enough to be in keeping with the setting.

Modern decor

Modern decor is always more difficult to define than traditional, but in the main it is less cluttered, with cleaner, bolder lines to the furniture, a lack of applied ornament in the way of carving or inlays, lighter-coloured woods such as pine, beech or limed oak and a conscious use of space and areas of plain wall with carefully thought-out colour combinations, either subdued, subtle or vividly emphatic (as on page 21).

Today we are very colour conscious and, what is more important, even the most modest home- or bedsit-owner is able to *get* wallpapers, paints, carpets and fabrics in the colour of his/her choice. This simply was not possible before World War Two on the scale that it is today and I well remember my mother dyeing fabrics, towels and tablecloths to try to get colour combinations she could never have

17 *A bowl of mixed roses in a very English setting with Georgian-style reproduction furnishings.*

18 *A profusion of summer roses and foxgloves on decorative library steps echoes the rose-patterned carpet.*

19 *Pine and pink tweed is complemented by foxgloves and hosta leaves in a tall, modern pottery cylinder.*

bought. Now the range of choice is vast at very reasonable prices. The paint colour cards, carpet samples or fabric swatches from any major manufacturer are an Aladdin's cave of colour. So matching, toning and complementing the colours of our interior decor has become relatively commonplace.

If flower arrangements are to play their own part as a feature of modern decor they should display the characteristics of present-day design. Many interior designers today use cut flowers packed into a vase or bowl simply as a mound of colour or texture, rather as one might use a cushion or a lampshade for a colour accent or for textural contrast. The flowers do not exist so much as flowers, but as another part of the design pattern. And very effective it is, too.

The flower arranger will go a little further, I feel, to draw attention to the interesting qualities of the plant materials, yet still try consciously to use simple lines, varied texture and bold forms, eliminating all but the essentials in a design. The pretty, trailing foliages, gentle grading of flower sizes and mixed and massed profusion will give way to a much more restrained choice of plant materials with perhaps no more than two or three different shapes and lines in any one arrangement.

Photograph 19 shows an exaggeratedly tall, slim, hand-thrown pot which links in colour with the pine dresser but has a rough texture to contrast with the smooth, polished wood. Five stems of foxgloves show their own interesting curves and five hosta leaves provide a different shape for emphasis. The mauve-pink bell-flowers link with, but do not exactly match the tweed fabric of the settee and the lampshade. The style of the arrangement is simplified but still fairly naturalistic, whereas in photograph 20 nature has been tamed and controlled to match the severe lines of the pale wood shelf unit.

The whole look of this room was bleached and neutral, except for touches of blue in the curtains and lampshade. To counteract what could have been a chilly look, the complementary colour was introduced. Dark bamboo canes cut in various lengths are fixed in bunches (held by rubber bands) on two pin-holders in a dark brown earthenware pot. Horizontal canes are threaded through holes in the sides of the pot. Two 'Whisky Mac' roses provide an accent of colour and a focal point, while two sprays of orange-ball buddleia echo both the shape and colour of the roses, to provide additional interest.

Wallpapers

Patterned walls can be both a pleasure and a problem for the home flower arranger. If the pattern is not too dominant there are no particular difficulties: the traditionally patterned yellow and off-white paper in photograph 21 gives added interest behind a buffet table-piece in apricot, yellow and white. The cherub container bears aloft white foxgloves, roses, *Alchemilla mollis* and day lilies, with peaches, apricots, apples and a few flowers and leaves piled in a dish below. A velvet-covered oval base unites the two arrangements. For a well co-ordinated look, this unifying base is important and so is the repetition of some of the same plant material in each container.

For many years in the 1950s and 1960s white containers were popular for almost any style or colour of arrangement, but today it is generally felt that a white container (of whatever sort) is too eye-catching and detracts from the arrangement itself, unless some white flowers are used, as here, or white china, perhaps, is a feature in the room. It is a good guideline but should not be regarded as a rule.

A very strongly patterned wallpaper, however, such as William Morris's 'Blackthorn', shown in photograph 22, *does*

20 The strong horizontal and vertical lines of the pale wood furniture are repeated in the cut bamboo stalks of the arrangement. The orange colour of the flowers is complementary to the blue of curtains, lampshade and carpet.

21 *A traditional buffet table-piece is given extra interest by the background trellis-pattern of a yellow and off-white wallpaper.*

22 *Massed honesty seedheads, fabric magnolia flowers and an abstract painting are set off by a strongly patterned William Morris wallpaper.*

pose problems (especially so in a photograph where all three-dimensional effect is eliminated). Quite a number of attempts were made at this one! The simple answer would have been to treat the flowers as a block of colour without featuring them individually. Provided one of the colours in the wallpaper was used the effect would be fine. But I wanted to try something a little more intricate and this was one answer in autumn.

The silver honesty pennies (*Lunaria annua*) were beloved of the Victorians and Edwardians and so had a period feel to accord with the paper, but, like the paper, they are fussy. The artificial magnolia flowers and their two buds were brought back from New Zealand (pulled stem-first into the leg of some laddered tights with feet and pantee cut off. This is an excellent packing tip learned from the Natal flower arrangers who use it for packing fresh foliage and air-freighting). The bold flowers provided the necessary strong, large shapes to counteract the fussiness. And what of the abstract print nearby? The 'mound of colour' arrangement might have been safer, but I think this works because the honesty seedheads are massed – and therefore simplified – and only one type of flower is used, without a change of colour.

Fabrics

Patterned fabrics present much the same problems as patterned wallpapers, but often they are used as curtains confined to one wall in a room, and can, if necessary, be avoided as a background to a flower arrangement.

The possible inspiration from the colouring or style of a fabric should never be ignored. A really effective decoration may only be possible at one season of the year, as in photograph 23, when one needs the profusion of late summer (unless resorting to artificial or painted materials) to do justice to the bold, poppy-patterned curtains in orange, cerise,

brown, white and lime. None of these colours may actually be matched by colours available from the garden, but a wide variety of pinks, reds and oranges in crocosmia, phlox, pelargoniums, roses and fuchsias is enough to give a toning effect. The more tints, tones and shades there are, the less true matching matters.

The style of the fabric pattern, although based on flowers, is not naturalistic, but simplified. It would be possible to echo this with a bold modern flower arrangement perhaps using crepe-paper or polyester fabric poppies, but with natural fresh flowers available, the aim was to create a light, uncontrived design. The container has a double opening which allows a smaller arrangement at the base, bringing the plant material and colour right down to two round fabric-covered bases (covered silver cake boards) which pick out the bright pink and orange.

A useful tip in maintaining the 'hot' colour look in such an arrangement is to minimize the amount of green foliage used. Green cools everything down and cancels out some of the warmth and vibrancy of the advancing colours. Use instead foliage with red, bronze or brown tints if you can get it, or leaves that have been preserved with glycerine to a tan, brown or near-black.

Photograph 24 also makes use of inspiration from a fabric. It is a bold party piece for a large modern flat, which would suit few other homes and certainly would not be everyone's idea of a flower arrangement. Yet it illustrates well the maxim that flowers should be in keeping with the style of decor and furnishings. A pretty basket of mixed flowers would have looked incongruous in this setting.

The polystyrene 'sculpture', painted with brilliant yellow emulsion paint is circled with white-painted wild clematis (old man's beard) vines. The inspiration for these came from the

23 *Bright mixed flowers accentuate the bold, bright colours of a modern curtain fabric.*

40

24 *Polystyrene 'sculpture' and bunches of daffodils make a striking display for a black and white setting in a modern flat.*

25 *A mass of lacy wayside flowers softens the geometric lines of modern furniture.*

fabric. Bunches of double daffodils, at their April-cheapest, give areas of similar colour but different texture – and a delicious scent. The flowers are held in bunches by rubber bands, and are in plastic beakers of water pushed into hollows scooped out of the polystyrene blocks. These blocks were packaging salvaged from a local building site, so the cost was no more than for the paint and six bunches of daffodils, yet the overall effect is striking.

The advantage of polystyrene is that it is virtually weightless and so not difficult to fix and support. The large piece of 'sculpture' is held by a 15 cm (6 in.) nail through the circular black base. The top piece with the hole is supported on a length of black-painted dowelling simply pushed into both blocks like a skewer. The disadvantage of polystyrene is that it clings to everything, so shaping and scooping out holes is best carried out clad in a plastic mac in the garden!

Furniture

Photograph 20 shows a modern flower arrangement to complement the blond wood shelving shown again in photo 25. You can see in the background how the decor is carried through to the dining area with blue as the only additional colour to beige and white. This time the beige colouring is repeated in a large stoneware vase and the white umbel flowers are sprays of hemlock (*Conium maculatum*) picked from the roadside verges.

Hemlock comes into flower in July just as wild parsley or Queen Anne's lace (*Anthriscus sylvestris*) is finishing. Although very similar it is much taller, reaching about 1.5 metres (5 feet), and the stem is easily identified by its purple-brown blotches.

The arrangement needs no supporting mechanics and although it will last but a day or two, has an artless simplicity which accords with the simple, clean lines of the furniture.

The large, colourful *pot-et-fleur* in photograph 26 gains much from being placed next to the attractive oriental screen, because the colours of one are echoed in the other. The grouping is planted in the lining of a brass-banded Georgian jardinière. The rooted plants form a permanent decoration and for special occasions cut flowers can be added in small containers of water pushed into the soil. Bright red gladoli give height to the design and matching gerberas add a round shape which is lacking elsewhere. This type of decoration can be almost any size, lasts especially well and is generally trouble-free to maintain. Cut flowers can be changed quickly as they fade, or omitted altogether. As a decorative feature in a room it is much more attractive than lots of separate pots of houseplants, dotted around on window sills, shelves and occasional tables. 'Big is beautiful' was never more apt than when applied to a well grouped *pot-et-fleur*.

FOUR
ACCENTING A FEATURE

For centuries wall-hung tapestries and paintings have been enjoyed as part of the interior decor of any home which could afford to have them. It is only since Victorian times, however, that cheaper reproductions have been available to those with more modest incomes and today's excellent colour reproduction techniques make it possible for good quality prints to be bought quite inexpensively. The quantity and quality of prints in the shops has probably never been better nor more varied. Several photographs in this book (9, 12, 13, 16, 17, 19, 22 and 33) show pictures as part of the wall decorations, but the next two concentrate on flower arrangements actually designed to go with a picture.

It may seem curious to suggest that one work of art can inspire another because it could be argued that if you put a flower arrangement next to a picture, each will detract from the other; which is why it seems to me important that if a flower arrangement is to stand by a picture, it must be related in some way – by the use of colour, texture, line or overall style the flowers should draw attention to the picture. Whether the viewer will actually look first, or most intently, at the arrangement or the painting will probably depend on whether he or she is first and foremost an arranger or a painter! But it makes the point of the importance of *linking* again – a studied attempt to guide the viewer to see what you want him to see, a composition of features in a room that will add to its character.

The paintings featured in the next two photographs are in very different styles. Photograph 27 features an impressionistic painting of a nude pulling a garment over her head. The blocks of colour more or less divide into groups of brown, green, white and yellow and the flower arrangement attempts to do much the same. The tall container (see also in photograph 19) has a knobbly decoration which echoes the brownish area on the left of the picture; the curve of the horse-chestnut 'sticky buds' repeats the line of the model's arm and the grouping of yellow and white daffodils repeats the yellow and whitish areas of paint. The green leaves play their own part. Even the marble table top repeats the brown colouring, but here with a smooth, shiny finish instead of a rough one as on the pot.

The painting of the vase of flowers in photo 28 is by Marcel Dyf, born at the end of the last century. The simple basket of massed flowers makes no attempt to copy the painting since the season was wrong (it was far too late for white tulips) but I have kept white flowers in much the same positions the painter gave them. The other flower colours have been picked up with different types of flowers. Although the picture is twentieth century, the room is Tudor with plaster walls and exposed dark oak beams (the fireplace can be seen in photograph 32) which is why I chose a simple basket as the container. It is 'lined' with a glass casserole dish and a firmly fixed block of foam provides support for the stems.

46

27 *A modern, impressionistic painting is complemented in line and colour by a lazy-S arrangement of 'sticky-buds' of the horse-chestnut tree, daffodils and mahonia leaves.*

28 *A twentieth-century flower painting is highlighted with massed garden flowers in similar colourings.*

29 *Artificial flowers have their place in today's centrally-heated rooms and are seen here with a collection of bric-à-brac in blue colourings.*

Ornaments

The Chinese lion-dogs of Fo normally sit on the radiator shelf in the hall on either side of the copper Art Nouveau-style letter rack, but it was not possible to photograph them *in situ*. So they were moved over to the mahogany cupboard which is probably late nineteenth century and with them I put an early nineteenth-century teacup and saucer, a Sèvres-style cup, a little Delftware chair and a Victorian pot lid. An eclectic grouping, but I console myself that the Georgians too were eclectic, borrowing freely from every age and culture to create their own style.

The flowers, of course, are frankly artificial; well, perhaps not altogether 'frankly' because one can easily be led, in the right season, into thinking they are real. I make no apologies for them. What else does one put over a hot radiator in winter that brings with it such a touch of summer? It is possible to emulate Madame de Pompadour who is said to have sprinkled perfume on artificial flowers placed in a winter garden. It is delicious, but expensive! The flowers are made up into five bunches and these are held in place by crumpled wire mesh pushed into the letter holder.

Ornaments and souvenirs from holidays or a visit overseas often make a decorative feature in our homes and this may be the inspiration for a flower arrangement as well.

30 *New Zealand basket shapes with an arrangement of dried native New Zealand flora provide a reminder of a visit to the other side of the world.*

31 *Pink double-flowering cherry blossom needs nothing added for a lovely display.*

Attractive New Zealand basket shapes by that most imaginative of basket makers, Ruth Castle of Auckland, inspired a grouping with some plant treasures brought back from a working visit there to give day schools. In photo 30, one basket shape hangs on the wall and the second (just discernible) is curved to hide a flat black dish fitted with a sturdy pinholder and a block of dry-foam. The plant material was arranged through the openwork basket and held by the pins or the foam. First were the pieces of black, weathered *Ponga* (the New Zealand tree fern) whose bold pattern and black/brown colouring surely helped to inspire the basket maker.

The furry white stems are the stalks of *Astelia* and the silver fern (emblem of the Maori rugby team) was pressed for me in Auckland. The glycerined eucalyptus leaves were grown in England but were very suitable, and the dried protea flower heads completed a grouping which so strongly evoked New Zealand that I could hear again the clipped-vowel accent and recall the kindness and hospitality of the flower arrangers in that country.

Since everything was dried and preserved it made a long-lasting arrangement in muted, restful colours, highlighted with silver.

Mirrors

Mirrors are such valuable ornamental features in rooms, giving the illusion of space and adding light to darker walls and corners. They often give an attractively new angle on some familiar object or aspect and they are certainly a most useful backing to a flower arrangement. A few flowers can be made to seem many more, provided one remembers the mirror while arranging. It is no good having a 'poor back' to the arrangement for the mirror is quickly going to show up any deficiencies. On the other hand, just one or two coloured flowers tucked in at the back of an arrangement will have much more impact.

Blossom time means that one can have a large jug or vase indoors to watch the unfurling of leaves and opening of flower buds. Cut the branches when the buds begin to show petal colour. It is really far too late when the flowers are nearly full out, as petals will soon drop in the indoor warmth and you will already have lost half the vase-life of the flowers and much of the pleasure. I find it best to *boil* the cut ends of any branches brought indoors for forcing in this way. Simply wrap the blossom buds in a tea towel to protect them from steam and hold the cut ends in an inch or so of boiling water for 30 seconds. Then arrange the stems in deep water. I rarely use any mechanics for the kind of massed vase arrangement shown in photograph 31; the comparatively narrow neck holds branches in place.

The double-flowering cherry grows at the bottom of the garden and we had it originally as a small seedling. Now it has to be pruned to reduce the shade it casts on the cutting garden. It goes well with the colouring in my sitting-room and I look forward to the couple of weeks each year when it can be enjoyed. It has never seemed easy to arrange with other flowers so now I don't even try.

Fireplaces

The fireplace this century has led a chequered existence for which two things are responsible: central heating, which made it largely unnecessary, and television, which made it no longer the focal point of a sitting-room. The dancing flames were replaced by the flickering screen and the colourful glow by not very attractive radiators. Owners of older houses had fireplaces ripped out or blocked up and new houses simply did not have any. But we missed them, and insidiously fireplaces have crept back. Glowing logs and coals may often be synthetic, and the warmth produced may only be supplementary to that supplied by background radiators but the hearth in

33 Modern brick, quarry tiles and stainless steel provide a setting for a sparse, vertical design of hogweed stems and daffodils.

summer is again a place where flower arrangements can stand.

The brick-backed open fireplace in a Tudor room makes an attractive setting for an all-foliage arrangement in a glazed earthware pot standing on a three-legged stool to make it seem a little more important (photo 32). A branch of *Elaeagnus pungens* 'Maculata' makes the height and is backed up by ferns, including a hart's tongue showing boldly on the right, and several feathery types. Two kinds of euonymus provide variegated leaves as do hostas and ivies. The blue-green touches at the centre are a sedum in bud (upper left) and two rosettes of the invaluable Jackman's blue rue. Such an arrangement lasts a long time if mist-sprayed regularly with tepid water.

The brick fireplace in photograph 33 was in a quite different setting in a modern house with plain carpet and leather-covered furniture, so a very sculptural arrangement seemed called for. The huge, ridged, dried stems are those of the giant hogweed (*Heracleum mantegazzianum*)* which have dried to an attractive brown and beige. Each of the three tallest stems is impaled on a separate pin-holder fixed to a board hidden by a box lid covered in bright yellow felt. A large hole has been cut out to allow the stems to stand through. The shortest section of stem stands on top of the base cover with a 2.5 cm (1 in.) section to complete the grouping. The spoked seedheads, with end-florets cut away, are from the same plant (which has umbels of white flowers in summer much like its smaller cousin of the road-side verges). This construction can stand as a sculptural piece if wanted, but on this occasion a few daffodils were added at three levels, held in tins of water pushed down and wedged into the hollow stems. The daffodils can easily be replaced by other flowers as needed, or omitted altogether.

*It is an offence under the Wildlife and Countryside Act 1981 to introduce this plant into the wild.

Collections

I remember an article many years ago in *House and Garden* magazine entitled 'The Abiding Passion to Arrange'. It was not dealing with flower arrangement, of course, but with the arrangement of objects, ornaments and collections of things in the house. If memory serves aright the article suggested that either symmetry or asymmetry could triumph, depending on what one had to arrange and to a greater extent on whether these objects were in pairs or were disparate shapes and sizes.

In photograph 34, the little collection of Victoriana stands on a fretwork-backed walnut canterbury and is dominated by the oval, domed frame with a stuffed canary. It was my mother's pet canary and when it died in 1901, her taxidermist grandfather stuffed and mounted the bird for her.

The tall dome holds a dried arrangement and in front a 'hand' vase (a modern copy) is arranged with fresh pinks, ivy and narcissi. The red glass basket holds garden snippets of forsythia, bergenia, grape hyacinths, rosemary, the same pinks and narcissi and one or two anemones. The Victorians would have enjoyed just such a mixed bunch, in the same way that they would have approved the crochet mats beneath each container, but I am sure they would have had pairs of everything and would have set them symmetrically on either side of the centre. Two silver-topped scent bottles complete the group. It gave me pleasure to arrange my little bits and pieces and grouped together they were much more effective decoratively than dotted about the room.

Whatever you collect, whether it be matchbox tops, beer mats, glass animals, stamps, teapots, wine glasses, figurines or cigarette cards they can all be displayed for decoration in a visually attractive way. The secret is usually to *mass* them together in blocks or panels. Dotting them about gives no

real sense of a collection and fails to suggest its size and scope. Quite often it is possible to combine a flower arrangement with such collections, picking up some of the colours in the flowers, or perhaps using plants which have special associations with the collection. I am still trying to work out the best way of adding flowers to my daughter's collection of coronation and royal wedding mugs, which hang on individual hooks in blocks of 20 (four wide and five deep) on the staircase walls.

34 *A collection of Victoriana holds posies of small flowers in much the same way as the Victorians enjoyed them.*

FIVE

HIGH DAYS AND HOLIDAYS

Party time

Flower arrangements for a party can – indeed should – be larger, more striking and more eye-catching than one would expect to have about the house every day. Because there will be more people about, chatting in groups, moving round in the dining-room or sitting on the stairs eating a buffet lunch or supper, flower arrangements also have to be very stable or well out of the way of guests to avoid accidents. It is a mistake to think that they also need to have a great deal of money spent on them. Some of the most striking arrangements can be achieved at little cost.

The buffet table arrangement (photo 35) stands almost 1.2 metres (4 feet) high in a black modern pottery cylinder with two openings. The branches are from ash trees (*Fraxinus excelsior*) at a stage which often goes unnoticed. The distinctive black buds have burst into purplish-black flower clusters which precede the better known seedheads we call ash 'keys'. The colour links well with the black container but the very rough texture is quite a contrast. The New Zealand baskets (see also page 50) provide another colour and pattern link. Three brilliant, well-opened, scarlet and white tulips are echoed in the red, fabric-covered cakeboard base. A black cloth and striking paper napkins complete a bold party piece which could be adopted to suit all sorts of near-bare branches (apple, contorted willow or hazel, stripped ivy) and two or three bold flowers, real or artificial. The mechanics needed are two strong pin-holders, one secured in each of the two levels in the container.

Photograph 36 shows the value of getting party flower decorations up out of the way. The door could be locked as it was not in use and the inexpensive hanging baskets made excellent containers for mixed spring flowers, mostly from the garden but including a few bought from the florist. A small block of soaked floral foam was taped onto a plastic saucer secured with wire onto each basket level. Sprays of white bridal wreath (*Spiraea arguta*) and variegated ivy trailed gracefully from each tier with the more solid colours of polyanthus, narcissi, grape hyacinths, daffodils, tulips, wallflowers, flowering currant, hellebores and freesias clustered in each basket. The roses are artificial.

These tiered baskets have been used again and again: hanging in a bay window holding tumbling roses in their midsummer profusion; at Christmas with holly, ivy, baubles and small artificial red poinsettias; in autumn with old man's beard, berries, apples and pompom dahlias and also arranged entirely with dried seedheads, glycerined leaves and cones and beech mast cases wired into sprays. For the party-giving hostess it is so valuable to be able to leave the table and other horizontal surfaces free, and to have flowers placed high where they can be seen throughout the party.

Easter

The movable feast of Easter, coming sometimes at the end of March or up to four weeks later in April, means that we can seldom be certain what flowers will be available for arranging on Easter Sunday. Brilliant yellow forsythia and daffodils, the great stand-by, may be scarcely out – or over. But if you have a garden, however small, it is likely that it will furnish you with enough for a plate-garden. As you will see in photograph 37, such a garden makes an attractive coffee-table decoration and an assembly point for eggs and other Easter gifts for the family.

Make the garden in a deep meat dish, shallow tray or even an old-fashioned soup plate. I find sand a good foundation but peat, compost or earth will do as well. Spread about half an inch thick over the bottom of the container, then cover it with green moss. A little landscaping helps here, or variation in height can be gained using a piece of driftwood or one or two stones. A slightly asymmetrical design is pleasing, with a twig or two (in this case the newly-opening leaves of the common elder) some forsythia and flowering currant fixed into a half-buried well pin-holder to one side of the container. Other flowers or small plants can be in cut-off cigar tubes or small tins of water or even pushed through the moss into the sand itself in a hole poked out with a skewer or knitting needle. Keep the flowers and leaves small; scale is very important in preserving a natural look; use something too big and the whole illusion is destroyed. Daffodils, except the tiny rockery ones, are too large unless you are working on a really big version. The finished effect is rather like the sixteenth-century *mille fleurs* tapestries with their flowery meads besprigged with pinks, pansies, buttercups and daisies.

The plate garden is a scaled-down version of the popular landscape arrangement which is itself a scaled-down version of a real natural

35 *A striking buffet-table party-piece in red and black uses ash buds and wide-open tulips.*

36 *Spring flowers in tiered hanging baskets are effectively out of the way for a party.*

59

37 *An Easter plate garden is colourful and uses only short-stemmed flowers.*

scene. In a landscape arrangement the branch to make a 'tree' will be taller, and the flowers and leaves larger, but the scale relationship has to be watched in the same way. This is especially important if you are using figurines, animals or birds as accessories. They must be in scale with the scene being created, *and with each other* or the whole landscape looks incongruous and ceases to be pleasing.

Christmas

Decorating the house for Christmas is always a pleasure, especially if you plan ahead and don't leave everything until the last minute with the result that glitter gets into the Christmas cake icing and you find the shops have long since sold out of green and red paper napkins or gold spray. Whether one chooses to have fresh or dried, painted or artificial floral decorations is largely a matter of personal whim, but it also, I think, depends a good deal on one's decor and furnishings. If the house is traditional in style then fresh holly, ivy, red carnations and poinsettias are likely to be your choice, but even so some baubles, glitter and whitened fir cones may be added. If your decor is more modern then you may be likely to opt for more sophisticated and unusual colourings such as turquoise blue, bright cerise or subtle apricot.

38 *A curving Christmas table decoration in the style of Colonial Williamsburg in the United States of America.*

The idea of the Christmas table decoration in photograph 38 is borrowed directly from Colonial Williamsburg in the United States of America and details of how it is made came from *Colonial Williamsburg Decorates for Christmas* by Libbey Hodges Oliver, the flower supervisor there. It has been adapted slightly for English plant material.

The basis is a 25 cm (10 in.) wreath ring of floral foam in a circular plastic trough. This is cut in half, and one of the semi-circles is reversed to make an 'S' shape. Soak the foam very thoroughly. To protect the polished table I cut a similar slightly larger 'S' shape in thick transparent polythene on which to stand the container. Using plain and spotted laurel (*Aucuba japonica*) make a 'frill' all round the 'S' shape. If your table is not large, the leaves may have to be cut down to a half or two-thirds and this helps to keep the Hogarth curve shape manageable. With cupressus, box, holly, yew or any other available evergreen, roughly cover the remainder of the foam so that it does not show. I used artificial fruits and berries to add colour, with gilded cones and clusters of gilded walnuts (each drilled with a hole and given a stub wire 'stem'). If natural berries and small red apples are available then use these. The decoration repays you for a misting spray each day. It looks very sumptuous indeed. Candles can stand in the hollows of the 'S' if you wish or even in the foam of the arrangement itself. Many variations are possible, perhaps with dried and glycerined leaves and natural cones and nuts; or you could make a frosted and glittered version with everything whitened.

The Christmas 'pedestal' is actually the base of a Victorian table and the 2 metre (6 feet) high arrangement is well out of the way in a corner of the dining-room. The dark green outline sprays are of *Garrya elliptica* with their long grey-green winter catkins. The sprays of white and pearlized holly, the lime-green mahonia and green and white fir branches, are all plastic. Polyester flowers include red gladioli, carnations, a poppy and a rose and two shiny gold sprays of something which are effective, but strictly unrecognizable. Dried hydrangea heads are sprayed with car paint spray and one or two very large cones are whitened. Keeping to the traditional Christmas colours makes it all look very naturalistic, even though the choice of materials is widely varied.

If you can find room for it, one fairly large Christmas arrangement like this is much more effective than a number of small ones.

Conclusion

The arrangements in this book, covering the changing seasons and all kinds of different rooms, will give some suggestions for the flower arrangements you might have in your own home, but they will always have to be adapted to the colour and style of your home and your personality.

Ephemeral though they may be, flower arrangements in the home should look as though they 'belong'. They should not give the impression that you have gone to some trouble to make an arrangement and you want everyone to admire it, even if the colour doesn't fit in with the decor, the shape is wrong for the space it fills and the whole balance of the room is upset. Don't consider just the arrangement, consider the whole setting, and when you have done and put the arrangement in place, walk towards the door, look back (yes, several times) and appraise your handiwork as though you were entering the room for the first time.

If you get a pleasant thrill of 'rightness' because room and arrangement seem made for each other, the pleasure will stay with you for several days at least. It is one of the satisfying rewards of flower arrangement.

If, on the contrary, you have a nagging, niggling feeling that something is wrong, spend

39 *This showy, 2 metre (6 feet) high Christmas pedestal arrangement uses a mixture of fresh, dried, painted, glittered, plastic and fabric flowers, leaves and seedheads.*

a little time deciding why. Does the colour not quite tone, are the flowers too big, the container too squat, or does the arrangement need to be simpler in style? If you cannot decide what is wrong ask another member of the family or a friend, because sometimes we are too involved to see our own work objectively.

There is always another day, another season, another arrangement to be done, another combination to be considered and a new container to be tried out. The flowers you put in your home will express your personality just as much as your choice of carpet or curtains. Whatever they are, enjoy your flowers in every room.

63

INDEX

Numerals in italics refer to the numbers of colour illustrations